WRITING SUBTEXT

How to craft subtext that develops characters, boosts suspense, and reinforces theme

Booklet #1 in a series

Elizabeth Lyon

Writing Subtext

Copyright © 2013

ISBN: 978-1490429885

www.elizabethlyon.com

Cover image by Marilyn Mills, TwinWillows Design

Interior print layout by Booknook.biz

Dedication

For Carolyn J. Rose
who suggested this series
a friend through thick and thin
a person who inspires me
a writer who proves that it pays to never give up

With gratitude for the patience, pondering, and
encouragement of my brilliant critique group
friends: Barbara Corrado Pope, Faris Cassell,
Mabel Armstrong, Kari Davidson, and
Geraldine Moreno Black

With special thanks to
Sarah Cypher, The Threepenny Editor
Marilyn Mills, TwinWillows Design
and to the Redditt Foundation

Contents

"Your intellect may be confused, but your emotions will never lie to you."

—Roger Ebert, movie critic

SUBTEXT IS ONE OF THE MOST ELUSIVE AND POWERFUL elements of craft. Literally meaning what lies beneath the text, it is an undercurrent, a hidden agenda, a vibe, a reinforcement of theme—and it exists in what is implied but not explicitly spelled out. It has impact because what you don't say is often more powerful than what you do say.

No wonder it's hard to wrap our minds around subtext, much less know how to apply it in our writing. But the pay-offs for learning how to write subtext are great: believable characters with hidden, sometimes complex motivations; increased suspense created by pressurized undercurrents; and a strengthened and unifying theme permeating the fabric of your story.

Hans Christian Andersen's "The Emperor's New Clothes" is a fitting example, pun intended. In case you haven't read this children's story lately, here's a summary: Thieves masquerading as master weavers offer the emperor a litmus test to rout out slacker employees: the unworthy will not be able to see the fine new suit. The subterfuge is that while pretending to weave, the thieves stash the expensive gold threads and fine fabrics. First the emperor's ministers cannot see the glorious suit on the weavers' looms. They're incompetent! Their jobs are in peril. Then the emperor himself is shocked when he cannot see it. Is his Highness undeserving of his throne? Like a lot of people currying favor, all of his advisors lie: they pretend they see his suit and launch a cover-up (so to speak), everybody raving about the colors, fabrics, patterns, and beauty of the suit. Not daring to reveal that he is among the dolts who cannot see the suit, the in-the-buff emperor parades before his subjects. A child finally speaks the truth: "But the emperor has no clothes!"

As "The Emperor's New Clothes" unfolds, readers wonder when someone will say this truth, and bring the obvious into the open. Subtext suggests that the emperor is not only gullible, he is a fool. In the face of the "naked" truth the emperor doubts himself. Thematically, subtext suggests that it is human nature to go along and hide our vulnerabilities. We are all fools because we can all be fooled.

Although "subtext" may be new to some writer's, human experience is permeated with multiple layers of innuendo, interpretation, and meaning. Toddlers and young children take everything at face value. They must learn how to recognize the signs and symbols of hidden meanings. I'm sure some people catch on to subtext early while a small percentage never does figure it out. Others have an acute ability to "read" people—their body language, shifts in tone of voice, and the insinuations behind their words.

All of us have likely experienced stepping into a room of people where we sensed an unusual mood— something said that we weren't privy to. Perhaps we took a moment and noticed that no one was smiling; heads were bowed. We asked or thought, "What's wrong? What happened?" We decode the nonverbal messages enough to be alerted to the existence of subtext, even if it takes longer to decipher the meaning behind the "body language."

In close friendships and marriages, we send cues that escape the notice of outsiders. A shift in tone of voice, the lift of an eyebrow, a shrug of a shoulder. At some time or another, all of us have withheld what we were really thinking when talking with others, but we may not have been polished actors in hiding our true feelings. "Oh how beautiful! It's lovely. Thank you!" we say, but think *I've never seen such a hideous knick-knack.* Then the gifter, picking up some vibe, sees through the guise and says, "If you don't like it, you can exchange it for something else." So often what we think we're hiding is in plain sight. We humans run around making assumptions based on subtext we incorrectly or correctly interpret, while at the same time giving out covert messages. And so should our characters.

A Quick Review of Craft

To navigate the instructions for writing subtext, we all have to be on the same page with the terminology of the craft. If you feel on solid ground with your understanding of the basics, feel free to jump to the next section. Otherwise, here is a quick review of five primary elements of craft: *characterization, plot, story, narration, and theme.*

Characterization applies to major and minor characters, who must be developed in varying detail, with the most attention paid to characterization of the hero or heroine, i.e., the protagonist. It includes physical description, emotions, thoughts, and actions.

Plot provides forward motion through action toward resolving an important problem introduced in the beginning of a novel or short story.

Story is different from plot. Some teachers define *story* as synonymous with *plot*. In casual use it is. But it has a specific function in craft. Every work of fiction has (or should have) an external storyline, the plot, and an internal, psychological storyline, which I am calling *story*. Plot springs from story, and *story* reveals why the protagonist takes particular actions in the plot. The answer to why supports theme. For example: An unmarried woman becomes obsessed with adopting a Bulgarian orphan she fell in love with even though the country finds her marital status unacceptable. That outlines the plot. However, the same woman, whose mother abandoned her as a youngster, will stop at nothing to adopt the child who fulfills her own need for being taken care of. That explains her actions by supplying the internal, psychological story. Notice how the sentence describing the plot creates visual pictures; you can begin to conjure scenes. The sentence describing story is thematic; it conveys the underlying psychological need that drives the mother.

Narration, simply put, includes all forms of "telling," not to be confused with the word "narrative," which means "the story." Narration is a whopper category that includes information, description of characters and setting, flashback summaries, thought, and the "sad, mad, glad" emotions as well as the "fight, flight, excite" reactions. You may have heard the writer's mantra "show don't tell." Show means plot action and tell means narration. All together, you have produced the narrative of your story, told by narrators—the protagonist, other viewpoint characters, and sometimes the author. When used well, narration adds depth, but when overused, telling tempts the reader to skip portions of your book.

Theme is meaning, the message that readers contemplate before and after they finish the last word. Theme may be expressed in one word such as love or justice, or it may be expressed in a line such as "Redemption is only possible by forgiving oneself," or in the biggest cliché of all, "Love conquers all."

To summarize the elements of craft, your task in writing is to show goal-oriented characters with psychological motivations taking action in the plot; to describe the story world; to reach the plot goal; and to reveal the meaning of the protagonist's journey, through theme. Subtext delivers that meaning, increases the impact, and develops characterization. In the course of writing or revising a short story or a novel, you will see opportunities to build subtext using all five elements. More examples and techniques follow.

Overview of Text and Subtext

SUBTEXT EXISTS IN ALL FORMS OF WRITING. IT CAN BE obvious like all caps shouting at you in an e-mail message, or it can be subtle like a watermark on a sheet of paper. It can be as mundane as the reader thinking, "they're flirting; they'll become lovers, I bet," or as profound as "the sadness of this passage makes me aware that life is fleeting. I should savor every moment."

You're at your computer and the blank page recedes as you fill it with text—scenes with action, dialogue, character goals, and description. Readers might have suspicions about a character's "real" motives, they may anticipate what is going to happen, or they may feel a subtle but palpable undercurrent of fear or anger or passion, of intention or plotting or subterfuge.

Teachers, agents, and editors often tell writers that every story should be about "the thing and the other thing." Two sources of tension and suspense: from plot and from subtext. What is overt and what is covert. If there are multiple "things" happening between the lines, then you have that many more sources of tension, subterranean forces, thematic possibilities, and character motivations.

For most genres of fiction, a writer's first task is to grab reader attention with plot: "lights, camera, action!" And then, through gestures, character's associations, metaphoric language, or a host of other possibilities planted in the story, the writer must telegraph other levels of meaning. Like the illusionist David Copperfield, you can lure your audience to watch one hand while you palm a coin with the other. In the hands of a skillful writer, sub-text is magic.

Foreshadowing is often the engine that drives subtext. Foreshadowing whispers that something is coming. The reader registers the hints as signals about what form the subtext might take. For example: What will happen to the young woman who has left her apartment unlocked, the door ajar, and then decides to take a shower? Readers may worry on her behalf or even feel terrified. The unlocked door, ajar, foreshadows the subtext that she is in danger. In most stories, it will be a very bad guy, not a kitten, that pushes the door open. We've seen Hitchcock's film *Psycho*. When the man enters and subtext breaks the surface, readers gain confirmation of what they already suspect: the threat generated by the subtext and felt by the reader now becomes text, part of the scene.

Although all subtext is foreshadowing, technically not all foreshadowing is subtext. Instead, foreshadowing may be mere set-up for the plot. For instance, if a man slips an engagement ring in his pocket before meeting the woman he's been dating, the foreshadowing makes the reader think a proposal may be forthcoming. This action generates a little bit of suspense by raising questions: Will he actually propose and what will she say? During the scene when he and his beloved meet, anticipation grows over when, if, and how he will pop the question.

More character development connects foreshadowing to subtext. Suppose the man—let's call him Karl—feels uncertain about marrying Catherine. He's fifty-eight and never been married. Even as he pockets the engagement ring, he wonders if he'll feel trapped. He loves her and is frustrated that she won't settle for living together. The addition of this information still raises the same questions: Will he actually propose and what will she say? But with additional characterization, the reader has more reasons to care about the outcome. This vignette suggests ideas about commitment and the responsibility implied by taking a risk with consequences that last a lifetime. When and in what way he pockets the ring foreshadows plot action *and* raises questions about how Karl will resolve his ambivalence about this commitment. That's subtext to care about.

By character development, foreshadowing and subtext are linked in a meaningful way, but what about theme? To make your story unified and powerful, these four must be linked. Let's say the writer of the Karl story had in mind a theme of "power corrupts, absolute power corrupts absolutely." There is a problem: the proposal and Karl's ambivalence are disconnected from this theme. Foreshadowing is divorced from the most important use of subtext—reinforcing theme. If this was an actual story and Karl the protagonist, the writer should alter Karl's characterization (or change the theme).

To support the theme about power, what if Karl's motive for marrying Catherine—wealthy and heir apparent of an Oprah-size fortune—is not love but to acquire money to play in national politics, hoping to some day make a bid for the presidency? In a novel about power and corruption, the unity of plot with character and theme creates powerful subtext. After finishing the book, readers might consider the price of selling one's soul to the devil, the suffering of the many when greed replaces goodwill by those who are supposed to represent the people. Now foreshadowing and characterization are working in tandem with subtext and theme.

Because your job as a writer is to get your reader to suspend disbelief and enter the fictional world, also called the "fictive dream," foreshadowing seduces the reader into asking questions, needing answers, eagerly reading on. Depending upon your novel, this duo of foreshadowing and subtext can be playful, foreboding, entrancing, exciting, and so forth. A story that is only "lights, camera, action" may come across as superficial fluff like cotton candy, offering no sustaining suspense, little speculation about meaning, and for some readers no enjoyment. Even in plot-dominant novels such as thrillers, suspense, mystery, and adventure, the dynamic duo can replace the cotton candy with a rich tiramisu that leaves us wondering how the baker created so many layers of delicious flavor—as later excerpts from novels will demonstrate.

How to Begin

MY EXPERIENCE OVER THE LAST TWENTY-FIVE YEARS as an independent book editor and writing teacher leads me to believe that relatively few writers plan subtext before writing a first draft of their novels. It's a big enough job simply to finish it. A reader or an editor might spot subtext, bring it to the writer's awareness, and recommend that it be developed in revision. Some "pros" may write subtext into their first drafts; most writers will go back in revision and uncover possibilities using characterization, plot, story, narration, and theme. In other words, if developing the skill of writing subtext is new to you, you're a member of a very big club.

It is one thing to know the five basic elements of craft; it's another thing to stare at your writing and wonder what *specifically* you can do using narration, for instance. What is the writer's equivalent of building materials—wood, wire, cement, nails—to create the "house" of subtext? Further breakdowns into four categories will offer you tangibles to get started in revision:

- Character development (including physical reactions, gestures, emotions, personal histories, experiences, desires, thoughts, and speech)
- Nature (including flora, fauna, the seasons, and weather)
- Human-made "stuff"
- Mood and atmosphere

Character Development

SUBTEXT THAT *DEVELOPS CHARACTER* OFTEN CONSISTS OF hidden agendas and motives. A teenage boy is riding a city bus and being taunted by four gang members seated behind him. When a "blue-hair" woman using a cane boards, he gives up his seat and walks forward to stand in the aisle, holding onto an overhead bar. He's chivalrous, right? Respects his elders. The subtext suggests there are other motives, or perhaps only one motive: to put distance between himself and the gang members—damn whatever happens to the old lady. And another example: A twenty-five-year-old man dashes ahead of his shy co-worker, the one with luminous blue eyes, to chivalrously open the door. As he holds the door, his heart beats faster. The subtext: his attraction to his co-worker. The clues: dashing ahead, luminous blue eyes, his heart beating faster. What will happen? Is he attracted to her? You'd have to read on.

Nature

SUBTEXT THAT USES *NATURE* CAN FORESHADOW EVENTS beyond the control of the characters and become fodder for subtext. Rain might foreshadow cleansing and a fresh start, or it may foreshadow depression or oppression. Storms often foreshadow major change or danger. A chaplain on a battlefield gives last rites to a fallen soldier while the horizon line darkens and the sky fills with a rolling brown, possibly life-threatening sandstorm. The soldier is only aware of the chaplain and his wounds; the chaplain, the protagonist, is aware of his choice—to stay by the man's side or to leave for reasons we intuit or guess at, until the plot moves on and reveals his decision. The storm may offer subtext paralleling the inner turmoil of the chaplain's decision. If dramatic weather is used throughout the story, an author may be offering the reader thematic subtext about the enormity and possible calamity of making decisions when life is on the line.

Human-made "Stuff"

SUBTEXT RELATED TO HUMAN-MADE STUFF, IF ANIMATE, can operate in the story in the same manner as nature—as an uncontrollable force. Imagine that a crane being used for construction swings erratically over the unfinished top of a skyscraper. A safety inspector is absorbed in conversation with a construction foreman on the sidewalk below and vaguely notices the crane. Will there be an accident? The erratic crane and the people standing below it foreshadow that possibility. Is there subtext about the safety of our cities in a time of lax regulation?

If the objects of human-made stuff are inanimate, like a cityscape or a house, the writer may create subtext by using them symbolically. A village of palapas, huts with thatched roofs, could convey simplicity, closeness to nature, poverty, fragility, or a tight-knit community. Empty high-rise office buildings and condos in Shanghai might symbolize progress, excess, affluence, power, pride, and disconnection from nature. It all depends upon the story and its theme.

Mood and Atmosphere

WHEN *MOOD* OR *ATMOSPHERE* PERMEATES A SCENE OR story, it suggests subtext. It may leave the reader with an intuition or contemplation about its symbolic meaning. For example, imagine a fantasy that takes place in an underwater city of sentient sea creatures. The writer will depict the natural world, and because it will be "peopled" ("whaled"?) by ocean-related nouns and movement-related verbs, the mood will be reflective of the imagined sea world.

When the writer introduces something discordant to the established mood, the reader goes on alert. For example, what if a humpback whale (a point-of-view character) surfaces and sees waves that do not sparkle, where black, like the spew of a squid, spreads as far as her eyes can see? Adding this out-of-place black sheen to the example sends the reader into speculation about what it is. The subtext not only foreshadows revelation of whether the black spew is an oil spill, it also suggests social commentary about environmental degradation and its effect on all life on earth.

Types and Placements of Subtext

One technique for developing subtext in your own writing involves underlining or otherwise marking words and passages that do the front job of foreshadowing. Then, in revision, you can develop these possibilities through character development and your understanding of what themes you intend. In the next sections, I'll use excerpts from novels to point out specific words and phrases that work together to create the following types of subtext:

- Sexual Attraction
- Predator Menace
- Unaware Characters
- Naïve Characters
- In Dialogue
- In Setting

Sexual Attraction

MOST READERS CAN SPOT ROMANTIC OR SEXUAL attraction. This is one of the most common forms of subtext and I can't resist having some fun demonstrating it:

Imagine a divorcee, long past the statistical probability of getting asked out on a date. She has love handles. Wrinkles, cellulite, and surgery scars don't make her a strong candidate for Match.com. Besides, she's not looking for anybody. But the man who tends her lawn, fifteen years her junior, is friendly and, frankly, charming. He asks about her kids and grandkids. They both speak Spanish. Sometimes they have discussions about life that run deeper than the best ones she ever had with her ex-husband. The landscaper is probably just an easy-going, funny, pleasant, considerate, and might I pile on, sensitive and mature man who has seen her without makeup or a bra, and is still willing to give her the time of day. On a shopping trip, she finds herself humming songs from *The Sound of Music* and buying new clothes.

Even though this vignette is out of context to a larger story, some readers will pounce on the sub-text of romantic attraction after line one. And when a character is oh so not looking for romance, the subtext is that she'll find it, even if it works out differently than she'd imagined. A man who is "charming and friendly" is a billboard-size sign. In a suspense or horror story, those two words might make the hairs prickle on the back of the reader's neck. This dude might be a pruning shears-wield-ing axe murderer. They have everything in com-mon and she believes he gets her like no one ever has. Is he a conman, a nice guy looking for romance, or is he simply a nice guy? The reader might entertain all of these questions. At first, the woman seems oblivious or unconscious to the romantic attraction, which makes the possibility of dangerous undercurrents more powerful than what's visible in the plot. When she's humming "the hills are alive" and buying new clothes, the subtext here most certainly is attraction.

The example raises suspense in the form of a question. To find an answer, readers must keep flip-ping pages. In this example, romantic attraction is the obvious subtext. On another level, the vignette is heavy with portent: a reader may read all kinds of possibilities between the lines, far more than mere attraction. You can, but need not, dig deeper and contemplate what else might be going on with this woman. Is she lonely? Bored? Does life not feel quite right without a beau? Does she assume she'll be judged by her cellulite? What's her story? Such speculation may or may not be borne out. But the possibilities add richness to the story.

Predator Menace

PREDATOR MENACE, WITH HUMANS OR ANIMALS AS predator or prey, is also common in fiction. Instead of happy anticipation of attraction or pleasantries, readers should feel some form of fear and maybe revulsion.

A novel where sexual menace contributes to powerful subtext and social commentary is *The Girl with the Dragon Tattoo* by Stieg Larsson. A gripping technique occurs when characters are not really talking about what is going on or about to happen, but the reader knows full well—and fears it, especially when subtext foreshadows danger. The following excerpt eventually turns X-rated, and I'll stop short of that point. For understanding, the character Bjurman is a lawyer who has guardianship over his female ward, Salander, a teenager. In an earlier scene, Bjurman, imperious, has taken full control of her money, in contrast to her prior guardian who let her run her own affairs. In the most recent scene between them, separated by scenes in other characters' viewpoints, Bjurman has interrogated Salander about her sex life. When her computer needs replacement, she must meet with him and ask for money. As the excerpt opens, he stands behind her, massages the back of her neck, and fondles her breast. He's a predator. She studies the letter opener on his desk, which she could reach with her free hand. Of course, already the scene is loaded with foreshadowing. I'll italicize the words and phrases that further foreshadow greater danger to Salander.

> Bjurman moved back to his side of the desk and sat on his comfortable leather chair.
>
> "I can't hand out money to you whenever you like," he said. "Why do you need such an expensive computer? There are plenty of cheaper models that you can use for playing computer games."
>
> "I want to have control of my own money like before."
>
> Bjurman gave her a pitying look.
>
> "We'll have to see how things go. First you need to learn *to be more sociable* and *get along* with people."
>
> Bjurman's smile might have been more subdued if he could have read her thoughts behind expressionless eyes.

"I think you and I are going to be good friends," he said. "We have to be able to *trust* each other."

When she did not reply he said, "You're a *grown woman* now, Lisbeth."

She nodded.

"*Come here,*" he said and *held out his hand.*

Salander *fixed her gaze on the letter opener* for several seconds before she stood up and went over to him. *Consequences.* He took her hand and pressed it to his crotch....

I'll stop here. Notice how spartan Salander's reactions are as Larsson has written this mostly dialogue scene. He leaves room for the reader's thoughts and emotions in anticipation of the assault that is about to take place—but who will be assaulter and who will be victim? Also note that I did not italicize the last sentence, "He took her hand and pressed it to his crotch...." Because there, the menace is clearly text, part of the plot, the threat is no longer veiled.

Communicating social commentary through subtext allows an author to escape a soapbox lecture using a character as a mouthpiece. Larsson, the author of *The Girl with the Dragon Tattoo*, as a teenager, reportedly stood by and did nothing as three of his friends gang-raped a girl named Lisbeth. It may be fair to say he never got over his guilt, and this novel presents Swedish readers, and by extension all readers, with a commentary about violence toward women, and the apathy and corruption of the institutions that are supposed to protect those most vulnerable to exploitation.

Unaware Characters

Although a character may be unaware of "what lies beneath" the plot action, the author can let the reader in on the subtext to great effect. Tension builds as the reader wonders—in some cases worries—if, when, and how the character will realize what is really going on.

Bestselling thriller writer David Baldacci dishes up rich stories that produce riveting moments through deft use of foreshadowing that implies subtext. As *Hell's Corner* opens, the president of the United States gives Oliver Stone a spy assignment of immense importance to the security of the country. The next evening Stone is strolling in Lafayette Park across from the White House where a state dinner is ending and guests are exiting to their waiting cars. Stone wanders and reflects upon the statues of Revolutionary War heroes, remembering the long history of the park and savoring his own experiences there over the years. Then he is drawn to look where he believes counter-snipers must be located for the protection of the White House guests, after which he identifies a motorcade that will carry and protect the British prime minister.

Stone notices four other people in the park, one a woman sitting on a bench near a fountain. She was "dressed in black slacks and a thin white coat. She had a large bag next to her. She appeared to be dozing," which strikes Stone as odd. Next "he spied a man in a suit carrying a briefcase, his back to Stone while he appears to examine a statue." The third person Stone sees is "a short man with a large belly . . . just entering the park . . . in jogging attire, though he looked incapable of even walking quickly without collapsing from a coronary." Further, Stone observes that "what looked to be an iPod was strapped to a belt around his ample middle, and he had on earphones." Last, he sees a man who "looked like a street gang foot soldier, dressed in prison shuffle jeans, dark bandanna, muscle shirt, camouflage jacket and stomp boots." Stone thinks that this man, too, is "odd" since "gangers" seldom come to Lafayette Park due to heavy police presence.

Notice how even one word, *odd*, can put the reader on alert and foreshadow trouble brewing. Add "the large bag, the suitcase, the iPod, earphones, a street gang foot soldier." Why would these items be odd? They aren't necessarily. Baldacci uses foreshadowing to grab reader attention and create worry, to connect the words and create suspicion of danger, while he turns Stone into the "clueless" or unaware character. For example: "But Stone had not come here to think about those things. He had come here to see Lafayette Park for the last time. In two days he would be leaving for his month-long training session." Stone then savors more memories of times here, in particular about a ginkgo tree, and wondering whether it will still be here in ten centuries. Yet, the reader does not cast off thinking "about those things." Foreshadowing grows and nurtures the seeds of subtext.

Now Baldacci has seduced the reader not only into believing that the other people are probably up to no good, but also that Stone is in greater peril by tossing his concerns away. The prime minister's motorcade heads toward the park on its way to Blair House. Readers must wonder, is the prime minister a target? The park visitors spring into action. Baldacci takes Stone out of his state of unawareness when he sees the woman, now awake and on her cell phone, and the jogger taking too long for the distance across the park, stopping and "fiddling with the controls on his iPod." Then Stone comes face-to-face with "the ganger who seemed to be walking in quicksand, but not getting anywhere," and recognizing the telltale "bump in the material" of the man's jacket that indicates he has a gun. He watches the advance of the motorcade and begins to gauge the danger to the prime minister. These descriptions jack up suspense, and confirm that these visitors are anything but benign. Stone is now as aware as the reader of the danger. In a final stroke of plotting genius, a bomb explodes next to the Andrew Jackson statue that Stone had admired. Turning the page to read the first lines of the next chapter, Stone awakens in a hospital. He, not the prime minister, was the intended target.

This thriller's plotting offers the reader emotions in reaction to foreshadowed danger, yet there is another, deeper, thematic level of subtext. Not only does Stone think about—and Baldacci provide the reader—lengthy details of the tradition and history honored in Lafayette Park, he is nostalgic about "the good old days" of youthful protest. We live in times when there is no place, no setting, that is sacrosanct—not churches, temples, or mosques; not flags or signs, not archaeological sites or parks with historic statues. If we believed that the rules of civil society insulate us from individuals with destructive intentions, or uncontrollable and sometimes lethal behavior and weapons, then we are as blind as Stone was, if only momentarily. Who will win the 21st century battle—the predator humans fighting and killing each other or the "enlightened" humans protecting each other? Even a political thriller can stir deeper thoughts, should a reader want to explore them.

Naïve Characters

INNOCENCE, NAÏVETÉ, AND IGNORANCE SET THE STAGE for reader investment and emotion in what the characters don't, perhaps can't, know. Although any character can be cast as "out of the loop," characters who are children, have mental illness, brain damage, or mental limitations are most vulnerable. Lenny Small in John Steinbeck's *Of Mice and Men* is a hulk of man, unusually large, incredibly strong, and mentally disabled. Set near Soledad, California in 1935, the story opens with Lenny's friend and protector, George Milton, a lean intelligent man, leading the way through the countryside to their next work as migrant ranch hands.

Nearly every page of this tragedy is steeped in subtext. Lenny loves to stroke the soft hair of small animals. Within a few pages, we learn that Lenny has pocketed, and stroked to death, a mouse. George makes him give it up, but in a short while, Lenny finds another mouse that he fondles too roughly and it dies. With this start, the reader anticipates death and the inability of George to prevent Lenny from doing harm—and being harmed.

Soon after George and Lenny arrive at the ranch, the wife of the ranch owner's son visits the bunkhouse and flirts with the men, to Lenny's delight. One of the laborers, Slim, tells Lenny he can have a puppy from the new litter—when it can leave its mother. The weakest four have already been drowned. While Lenny is in the barn, manhandling his pup, George talks about him with Slim back at the bunkhouse, as follows:

"He's a nice fella," said Slim. "Guy don't need no sense to be a nice fella. Seems to me sometimes it jus' works the other way around. Take a real smart guy and he ain't hardly ever a nice fella."

George stacked the scattered cards and began to lay out his solitaire hand. The shoes thudded on the ground outside. At the windows the light of the evening still made the window squares bright.

"I ain't got no people," George said. "I seen guys that go around on the ranches alone. That ain't no good. They don't have no fun. After a long time they get mean. They get wantin' to fight all the time."

"Yeah, they get mean," Slim agreed. "They get so they don't want to talk to nobody."

"Course Lennie's a God damn nuisance most of the time," said George. But you get used to goin' around with a guy an' you can't get rid of him."

"He ain't mean," said Slim. "I can see Lennie ain't a bit mean."

"Course he ain't mean. But he gets in trouble alla time because he's so God damn dumb...."

Subtext permeates not only this excerpt but the whole novella. The reader fears that Lenny will accidentally kill his puppy (he does) and fears that he will cause something bad to happen to the wife (he does). The plot foreshadows these fears, yet in the lines above, the men aren't talking about Lenny's danger to the puppy or to the wife. Beneath this spare prose run several strands of subtext. Through George, the reader might think about the loneliness of life, the friendships of convenience that take the edge off of despair, and the ambivalence involved with them. As well, this novella strikes deep emotional chords over the mistreatment and murder of the mentally disabled, and offers contemplation about ignorance, lack of education, and harsh times—then and now.

Many other questions arise from Steinbeck's story: What happens when people are doing the best they can with their circumstances and yet their actions cause others to die? When George kills Lenny, is it as expedient and necessary as killing the weakest puppies in the litter? What is inhumane and humane? What happens when people take the law into their own hands? Do harsh times justify harsh, cruel, and deadly actions? *Of Mice and Men* is a story that continues to deliver powerful subtext long after closing the book. In fact, in the best stories, it is often only after readers finish reading that the full emotional impact of the "story beneath the story" hits them. And that's why aspiring writers should expect that it will take thought, planning, and revision to create that impact.

In Diaologue

SOME WRITERS MAKE THE MISTAKE OF THINKING THAT writing for young children is easy, and that the storylines are so simple they would not have subtext. Both of these assumptions are incorrect. Although young children may not be able to articulate subtext, if indeed they detect it, the addition of it can elicit feelings that directly relate to an important theme. Authors of children's literature know that their books are likely to be read first by librarians, teachers, and parents, and finally by the children. After reading some books, adults can initiate a discussion about the book's deeper meaning and relevance. Often in children's literature, dialogue is more prevalent than narration and must include subtext between the lines.

Canadian author Lois Peterson writes novels for young children. In *Meeting Miss 405*, the protagonist, Tansy, has no say in her Dad's decision that she have an after-school sitter. He must work and her mother is away being treated for depression in an out-of-town hospital. Tansy's father takes her to meet the sitter, Miss Stella in apartment 405, whereupon Miss Stella offers them ice tea.

> "That would be nice," says Dad.
> "Tansy?" Miss Stella makes a puffing noise as she gets up. Just like Grandpa.
> "I'm not thirsty."

While Miss Stella is in the kitchen, I ignore Dad's frowny look. I run my fingers through the stack of paper. I love popcorn, but I'm not hungry enough to grab a single kernel.

Miss Stella comes back holding three glasses. Like a waitress, with two in one hand. She puts one on the table in front of me. "Some for you. Just in case."

In case of what? "This is red," I say. Iced tea should be brown. With a slice of lemon squatting on the rim of the glass.

Lemon I could give to Mom if she was here. Dad and I despise citrus.

"It's Roy Bus," she says. "Not tea at all, really. But delicious."

Roy who? I want to ask. But I am not talking to either of them....

"So, how will we get on, you and I?" asks Miss Stella.

I shrug. *Beats me*, is what I want to say. *This wasn't MY idea....*

Clearly, the subtext reflects Tansy's unhappiness and resistance to being taken care of by Miss Stella. (By the way, if you don't know what "Roy Bus" is, I didn't either. It's a "bush" tea made from the leaves of a legume grown in South Africa.) Most elementary school kids easily understand Tansy's reactions to being "baby-sat" by an old woman in their apartment complex. The child reader will likely identify with Tansy's anger and powerlessness. The subtext is not terribly veiled. However, in this passage, Peterson's subtext runs deeper because it resonates with the novel's themes of how a young girl copes with the absence of her mother, and under the unusual circumstance of emotional illness. In an earlier passage from this same scene when Tansy first meets Miss Stella face to face, another strand of subtext is revealed, as follows:

> Miss 405 is very old. And she is wearing shiny green shorts! I stare at her tanned wrinkly skin, which goes all the way down her legs in little ripples. Right to her bare feet.... I never knew knees could be bony and wrinkly at the same time. I don't want to look up. Maybe Miss Stella's face is all pleated like a turkey's neck....
>
> Her face is as brown and wrinkly as the rest of her. Like those rust-colored cliffs in the Fraser Canyon with ridges where the rain has run through. Her eyes are light blue. As if the color got washed out. Maybe she stood too long on her balcony in the rain....

This strange, at first off-putting, old woman mirrors how Tansy's world has flipped upside-down, and is thrusting her into new and challenging situations. As the story unfolds, Tansy learns that Miss Stella doesn't have a computer, TV, or peanut butter. She does calligraphy (which Tansy eventually tries and enjoys). At one visit Miss Stella is wearing a silk kimono with a colorful dragon that she painted onto the back. In other words, Miss 405 is different from anyone Tansy has ever met. As she is forced to spend time with her sitter, Tansy not only learns resiliency in response to crisis and change, she explores, thrives, and grows. Parents and teachers who read this book appreciate the subtext. They hope that children who have gone through a difficult patch in their lives will vicariously hitch a ride with Tansy. What makes *Meeting Miss 405* such a moving work, for all readers, is Lois Peterson's skillful building of subtext, at first revealing Tansy's insecurity, loneliness, confusion, anger, and worry, and then her acceptance and appreciation of Miss Stella with the discovery of the importance of finding someone you can trust.

In Setting

NOT ALL SETTINGS LEND THEMSELVES TO SUBTEXT OR relate to a theme. In those stories where it does, the setting itself may be so powerful it becomes a character and reinforcement of theme. Consider the Dust Bowl in Steinbeck's *Grapes of Wrath* or the decimated post-apocalyptic landscape in Cormac McCarthy's *The Road*, both novels sharing themes about survival, humanity and inhumanity.

Acclaimed historical mystery author Barbara Corrado Pope likewise selects settings that offer

subtext to her novels set in the latter years of 19th-
century France. Her detective is Magistrate Bernard
Martin. In *Blood of Lorraine*, he is presented with a
case of the brutal murder of a Jew's baby, setting
the stage for a novel that explores anti-Semitism in
France just before the trial of Captain Alfred
Dreyfus. As Pope describes Martin's transit through
the city of Nancy on his way to the morgue, more
than description is communicated to the reader, as
follows:

> Martin exited through the main entrance of
> the Palais de Justice which lay on the southern
> edge of the sedate and dignified Place de la
> Carrière. He loved the "Carrière" because it
> expressed in greenery and stone everything he
> believed in his heart, that progress, equality, and
> justice were possible. Part of the oldest section of
> the city, the stately elongated public square had
> once been a feudal playground for military
> parades and jousting, rimmed by palaces inhab-
> ited only by men of title and privilege. In the last
> enlightened century, the good Duke Stanislas
> had changed all that, harmonizing façades of
> surrounding buildings, acquiring some of them
> for governmental functions, and transforming
> the central strip into a park open to all, graced by
> straight rows of clipped linden trees, stone
> benches, and elegant statuary.

In this excerpt, Martin reflects upon and takes comfort in the principles of "progress, equality, and justice" that he sees reflected in the city's buildings and parks. This part of town still projects affluence and power. The novel carries the reader through unequal social classes, where privilege is no insulation from religious intolerance and Martin must overcome his own assumptions to deliver justice. Martin's reaction to the orderly setting mirrors his naïveté about the rising foment against the Jews. He looks at the old city center and sees stability and harmony brought about by a nobleman from the enlightened last century. His investigation is about to take him away from the light and into the dark quarters of the human heart.

Why Symbolism

THEMATIC SUBTEXT RELIES UPON SYMBOLISM. WE LIVE in a symbolic world. Words are symbols. I can just imagine Adam and Eve deciding upon names as they went around putting the first Post-It notes on everything in Eden. In my comic version, they broke up when they couldn't agree on how to label ideas—and emotions. Seriously, our words have literal meaning and symbolic meaning. Take the quotation, "A rose is a rose is a rose." Is it literal? Are we talking about the flower called a rose, or is it symbolic; meaning that the word "rose" and/or the entire phrase is a stand-in for some other meaning? In my ignorance, I had always taken this famous line to be a Zen koan, a mind-bender to bring one's attention back to "be here now." In actuality, Gertrude Stein quilled this line, referring to a person in her poem *Sacred Emily*. Later she used it as a one-liner, said to mean "Things are the way they are," which is pretty Zen to me. According to the ultimate reference on all things, Wikipedia, "In Stein's view, the sentence expresses the fact that simply using the name of a thing invokes the imagery and emotions associated with it."

A reader's understanding of subtext depends upon many things: his or her associations between literal meanings and symbolic meanings, which is likely also affected by nature, genetics, and nurture, upbringing. My father lives in a highly literal world and I enjoy a richly symbolic one. I discovered this when I was fourteen and had read Robert Frost's *Mending Wall* in my English class. I was enthralled with its simple beauty and spouted all the symbolic meanings at supper. I handed him the poem and waited until he had read it, or at least some of it. As a refresher, it begins:

> Something there is that doesn't love a wall,
> That sends the frozen-ground-swell under it,
> And spills the upper boulders in the sun,
> And makes gaps even two can pass abreast.

And at poem's end:

> He moves in darkness as it seems to me—
> Not of woods only and the shade of trees.
> He will not go behind his father's saying,
> And he likes having thought of it so well
> He says again, "Good fences make good
>   neighbors."

Discussing Frost's poem set off the first of few arguments I've ever had with my dad. "It's just a wall!" he said over and over. "No it's not, Dad, it's full of symbolism," I said, voice rising. He dug in. We went round and round, and when I stopped trying to convince him otherwise, there was a new wall between us, or my first realization that there had been one there all along.

Many of the examples already given in this booklet include symbolism that is part and parcel of subtext and is decoded in relation to theme. *Hunger Games*, by Suzanne Collins, was written for young adults and crossed over into adult readers. This first, bestselling novel in a trilogy is set in a dystopian, post-apocalyptic future where children must kill other children or be killed. The Games were invented by a sadistic, decadent totalitarian regime as a condition of surrender in a war against 12 districts. The entire novel is a terrific example of subtext used at many levels, especially through symbolism. The protagonist, a girl named

Katniss, is the first-person protagonist and narrator:

> Separating the Meadow from the woods, in fact enclosing all of District 12, is a high chain-link fence topped with barbed wire loops. In theory, it's supposed to be electrified twenty-four hours a day as a deterrent to the predators that live in the woods . . . . But since we're lucky to get two or three hours of electricity in the evenings, it's usually safe to touch. Even so, I always take a moment to listen carefully for the hum that means the fence is live. Right now, it's silent as stone. I flatten out on my belly and slide under a two-foot stretch that's been loose for years.

Is the reference to "the fence" just "a fence is a fence is a fence," or is it foreshadowing and symbolic? Just a few pages into the novel, as this excerpt is, the reader can guess but not know. If it is subtext, the symbolism will be cumulative, becoming more evident through repetition throughout the novel. Sometimes you can spot potential subtext by the amount of development given to it. Collins's description of the fence is far in excess of anything else *at this moment*.

If the author intended mere description, she could have written: "Katniss slipped under a loose stretch in the chain-link fence." The best authors make every word count. In revision, they prune out what is irrelevant, leave what is meaningful, and develop what they want readers to engage in fully. Collins has devoted a good portion of one page to the fence. Will there be an encounter with predators? Will there be a scene of electrocution? Will there be a need for Katniss to slip through the stretch that has been loose for years? All three bits of information foreshadow life-threatening events— in the plot.

We learn of a district demarcated by live barbed wire-topped high fences. The people who live in the district are prisoners, even if they have been told it is for their own good—as protection from predators. But at least one young woman has figured out how to gain freedom, and has dared to defy authority. The subtext is the life-and-death quest for freedom from a powerful, deadly regime.

When a novel transcends the typical reaches of its readership, becoming a blockbuster, usually the story taps into a collective need of its readers. They invest deeply in the protagonist's success because they share her need and suffer from deprivation of that need. Why did today's youth, and then readers of all ages, connect with *The Hunger Games?* Think student debt for life. Think minimum wage jobs. Think mortgages underwater, bankruptcies, food banks, and subjugated masses, while resources are funneled to an elite. Who's making money off the backs of students and common folk? This is the narrative that readers may bring to the *Hunger Games* and one reason why the powerful subtext has such great meaning. We began with but one paragraph, one symbolic object: an electrified fence. Taking this symbol's subtext to a deeper level of characterization, what is really going on inside Katniss—and the readers? The need to be in control of our own lives.

Using Imagery to Create Symbolism

IMAGERY IS PART OF WHAT IS CALLED "FIGURATIVE speech"; in short, comparisons of one thing in terms of another. Writers create imagery using similes or metaphors. Similes make the comparison using phrases that begin with "like" or "as" or "resembles" while metaphors replace one thing with another. My friend Jerry, in stature and strength, is like Paul Bunyan. I call him my rock. First a simile and then a metaphor. Similes and metaphors always ask the reader to do mental work and replace the image with the literal meaning. Think about the imagery we use in everyday life: He was as tired as an old dog. Her thoughts came as clear and fast as a spring stream. An effective simile or metaphor not only describes a person or situation, it requires no translation.

Conscious selection of imagery for symbolism allows you to lay down the tracks of subtext. Just one line of imagery can capture the theme of an entire novel. Carolyn J. Rose, a bestselling e-book novelist, created such a line in her mystery *Hemlock Lake*. In this story, Detective Daniel Stone's wife drowned and his brother took his life. After a year away, Stone returns home in an isolated community of Hemlock Lake in the Catskills. Feeling emotionally isolated and still grieving, Dan thinks that the friends and neighbors he has known since birth are wary of him, made worse by his assignment to investigate threats and arson related to the encroachment of a development of luxury homes.

A rattler that appears to have been intentionally placed under a jacket in his truck has bitten Dan. While the doctor is saving his life, the rest of the town folk are at a Memorial Day picnic. His love interest, Camille, herself an outsider, tells him that the town's women were "stewing about the state of your health and eating habits, while the men were determined to get 'the son of a bitch who'd do a thing like that to Dan.'" His ironic thought, conveying subtext: *Usually when folks consort with a snake they're booted out of the garden, not welcomed back.* This line, literally related to the rattler, cleverly symbolizes the theme of the mystery about the clash between long-time residents and newcomers, and more deeply about tradition and change and how people's reactions to both can reinforce what is good about human beings and expose what is evil.

One technique for developing symbolism is to comb through your story and make a list of repeated objects, colors, weather and seasons, emotions, circumstances, and emphasized or repeated words and phrases. Repetition adds emphasis and tells the reader that something is important. We tend to have collective agreement on the meaning of colors, for instance, but you need not conform to stereotype. Change a color from one you wrote unconsciously to another one that contributes to the meaning you wish your story to impart.

The color red is associated with fire, anger, passion, alarm, danger, emergency, speed, blood, love, vitality, and sex. How can you take this symbolism and create subtext? What if an emotionally numb character frequently flicks on a lighter or lights wood in a fireplace, or, reversing the meaning, has trouble getting a light or starting a fire? What is the symbolism, the meaning in the subtext? The character who repeatedly successfully lights a fire may be seeking rebirth or to kindle passion. In a story with an emotionally shutdown character who fails at starting fires, the writer has an opportunity at the climax to reverse the tragedy by showing this character's success at starting a fire, a big fire. This, of course, is my free association from the color red to fire to a character to a deeper meaning. Look at what colors you may have unconsciously used and decide if you need to repeat the colors more often or change them. Then revise to let the reader connect the context with your meaning. That's subtext.

You can do this same exercise with any object of importance. There will be a different symbolic meaning if an old geezer is driving a banged-up old Ford station wagon versus a brand new, gold-flecked Maserati. Ordinary objects are so often recognized (and used) for their symbolic meaning that they offer us ready-made subtext. Take this Rorschach test of mine—what are your associations to the following things: doll, key, door, bread, puppet, balloon, and clock? What symbolism can you attach to each item—and to the items or objects in your story?

Weather and seasons are full of symbolic potential. Gray skies, thunder and lightning, drenching rain, or a windless day all offer foreshadowing and subtext. Full moon, dark moon, sunny day, sunset, sunrise, high noon. Spring, summer, fall, winter. If you've included weather, time of day, and seasons in your story, will your reader intuit the subtext?

Unintended Subtext

SOMETIMES A CHARACTER BECOMES THE MOUTHPIECE for an author's morality lesson, epiphany, or axe to grind. In this case, the message is forced upon the reader in a way that takes advantage of the reader's open state while in the fictive dream. Unless the material is entirely in character, the subtext shows the author intrusion, unintended subtext, as clearly as a food stain on a shirt. As my editor friend Sarah Cypher has said so well, "The writer has hijacked the novel's subtext to deliver a message about the outer world." To clarify, you may be writing a novel about an issue or idea about which you feel strongly. That's fine—if you allow your character-driven story to reveal it, and develop subtext to support it. If you feel a strong urge to persuade a reader to a position or belief, then ask a friend or fellow writer to read what you've written and let you know if you've elevated yourself on that soapbox.

A different type of author intrusion may resemble subtext but is instead a deficiency of skill. It is so common that I want to mention it here. Writers often think they can stack big loads of information on the backs of dialogue. Without knowing it, they stomp all over the dialogue distracting the reader who instead ponders the tracks of Big Foot. The evidence of the author comes across like subtext, only in that it adds awareness of a writer's motive (to emphasize or to add information). What's between the lines is the author, not character motive or theme. It happens to all of us who write fiction. Here is a made-up and exaggerated example:

"If it isn't Fred Smith! I never expected to see you shopping in the diaper and formula aisle. Do tell?" Charlie called, pushing his cart toward his old friend. Their folks had lived next to each other in the south hills of Eugene from the 1970s on. Charlie and Fred had actually met in the sandbox in kindergarten.

"Hi Charlie White. You remember that gal I was seeing—Charlene Wilson? Well, we are the proud parents of a boy, Samuel Roman Smith, age 14 months." Charlie pumped Fred's large hand and slapped him on the bony shoulder. Fred was 6'4", had curly black hair, a tanned complexion, wore John Lennon-style glasses— still, and today had on a Go Ducks t-shirt and gray sweatpants.

"I haven't seen Charlene since we were at University of Oregon majoring in computer science. Is she still 5'6", a brunette with dark-brown eyes?"

This example demonstrates what I find in almost all novels I edit, to one degree or another. The writer has a long list of information to impart to the reader and lacks the skill to weave the information in where it belongs and in a way that hides the author's hand. Instead, dialogue gets loaded up with an "info dump."

Novels with Less Subtext

TO BE GOOD, EVEN GREAT, NOVELS MUST CONTAIN well-developed subtext, right? And you should feel like a shallow person if you can't find, or create, the kind of subtext that joins plot and character with theme? I suspect it will be a huge relief for me to tell you . . . no. Many writers have entertaining and engaging novels that may only display what I think of as "subtext-lite."

One such light-hearted novel that was also made into a Lifetime movie is *On Strike for Christmas* by romance/women's fiction novelist Sheila Roberts. I was quickly hooked by the women of the town of Holly and their boycott of doing any and all of the work that goes into producing the family Christmas celebration. Roberts makes many references to Christmas Past, Christmas Future, bah-humbug, and Scrooge. There is no subtext because the viewpoint characters openly discuss the comparisons. In one couple's argument, Joy confronts her "bah-humbug" husband:

> He [Bob] grumped his way through all the season's activities. The annual neighborhood Christmas party, New Year's Eve—whatever it was, if it involved a group of people and a good time Bob approached it like a man headed for the electric chair.
>
> "Show up?" she retorted. "You're a ghost. You may as well not be there."

A few paragraphs later:

> What happened to the man who, when they were first married, helped her trim the tree and sat next to her on the couch in her brother's living room and sang Christmas carols? He'd disappeared like the Ghost of Christmas Past. And,

somewhere along the way, this soured version of Bob had moved in and taken over.

A few paragraphs later:

> Bob gave a shrug. "We all experience that in different ways. And just once I wish the Grinch would steal Christmas."
>
> Joy crossed her arms over her chest and fumed. Bob Robertson, direct descendant of Ebenezer Scrooge. It was a good thing he wasn't in charge of Christmas.
>
> Wait a minute. What if he was?

Sheila Roberts makes ample and humorous use of the metaphor of Dickens's *A Christmas Carol*. Nothing is hidden. There is, however, subtext-lite in the immediate interactions of the characters in the plot. For instance, when reporter Rosemary Charles arrives with her photographer, Rick, to interview Laura, one of the women on strike, there is easy-to-decipher subtext, which I'll italicize, in Rick's reactions:

> "So what will he [Laura's husband] be doing?" Rosemary asked.
>
> Laura began ticking off chores on her fingers. "Putting up the tree and decorating, baking, doing the Christmas cards, cooking Christmas dinner."

Next to Rosemary, *Rick's mouth fell open.*
"Shopping, wrapping presents," Laura continued. "Oh, and he needs to make the costumes for the kids' holiday performances."
"Costumes?" *Rick squeaked.*

Roberts writes one line about the reporter that has crystal-clear subtext: "Rosemary Clark suddenly looked like a puppy that had been promised an entire bag of doggy treats." Metaphorically speaking about this simile, this reporter was an eager beaver. The imagery has no connection to the whole novel. It's spice but not the main course. Throughout the novel, little reactions, facial expressions and gestures, convey the undercurrents between the sparring couples and contribute to the humor. But notice that without these small touches of subtext, the characterization and humor fall flat and the dialogue is a mere recitation of facts. This and other novels suffer not at all from less subtext.

Pulling It All Together

THE ALPHA AND OMEGA OF SUBTEXT IS THEME. YOU may not have begun your story with theme in mind, but you do need to end up with one to have a viable story. Writers often have to ask someone else to figure out the theme, or to start with one and end up with another. What is your story *really* about? Not the blow-by-blows of plot but the message that corresponds with your hero or heroine's need, be it for revenge, love, forgiveness, identity, equality, understanding, or some other universal need.

With theme in mind, find places where your characters have or could have hidden agendas. Determine what they are holding close to the vest that they are unwilling to reveal openly. Read between the lines of dialogue or write lines that imply meanings other than what is spoken. Think about how you can add an undercurrent of emotion and plant a surprising revelation. Plan multiple revisions for developing the subtext of attraction and danger, anticipation and doubt. Consider your theme as you add details of setting and develop symbolism.

Subtext may have been difficult to grasp at first. Writing it takes practice. Your readers will love it when subtext becomes text and they can say, "I knew it all along."

~ ~ ~

WRITING SUBTEXT

Other books written by Elizabeth Lyon:

Manuscript Makeover
The Sell Your Novel Tool Kit
A Writer's Guide to Fiction
A Writer's Guide to Nonfiction
Nonfiction Book Proposals Anybody Can Write
National Directory of Editors & Writers

List of excerpts and examples:

The Girl with the Dragon Tattoo by Stieg Larsson
Hell's Corner by David Baldacci
Of Mice and Men by John Steinbeck
Meeting Miss 405 by Lois Peterson
Blood of Lorraine by Barbara Corrado Pope
Hunger Games by Suzanne Collins
Hemlock Lake by Carolyn J. Rose
On Strike for Christmas by Sheila Roberts

About the Author

Elizabeth Lyon, a freelance book editor, instructor, conference speaker, and author, began her career in 1988 teaching dozens of writing and publishing classes and workshops through Continuing Education at Lane Community College in Eugene, Oregon. She led three critique groups of writers on a weekly basis in her home for thirteen years. By consulting with writers, editing their whole or partial books, queries, synopses, and proposals, Elizabeth has participated in the publishing success of many nonfiction books, novels, 'indies' (self-published books), and contest winners.

The author of six books for writers, Elizabeth's last book, *Manuscript Makeover: Revision Techniques No Fiction Writer Can Afford to Ignore,* was featured in *The Writer* magazine as one of the "8 Great Writing Books of 2008," and described as "perhaps the most comprehensive book on revising fiction."

She lives in Springfield, Oregon. For details about editing services, client successes, and to sign-up for announcements of future booklets, contact: www.elizabethlyon.com.

33341330R00034

Made in the USA
Middletown, DE
09 July 2016